D0881636

TRANSITIONS, —— TRUST,——
—— *and* ——
—TRIUMPH—

A Daily Devotional for Caregivers

Jean D. Moody-Williams

WESTBOW
P R E S S
A DIVISION OF THOMAS NELSON

ISBN: 978-1-4497-5334-4 (e)
ISBN: 978-1-4497-5335-1 (sc)

Library of Congress Control Number: 2012908915

WestBow Press books may be ordered through booksellers or by contacting:

WestBow Press
A Division of Thomas Nelson
1663 Liberty Drive
Bloomington, IN 47403
www.westbowpress.com
1-(866) 928-1240

Printed in the United States of America

WestBow Press rev. date: 6/12/2012

TRANSITIONS,
TRUST,
and
TRIUMPH

Thanks to Danielle and Nicole Williams for the book cover concept that reminds us of a quiet and peaceful presence.

Introduction

She was enjoying the time of her life, shopping in New York. Little did she know that only three weeks later she would be unable to move her legs, dress herself or provide even minimal activities of daily living. This was the fate of the strong woman that provided care for me all of my life. With little notice, I found myself responsible for her care. I watched, and participated as she **transitioned** from independence to dependence, as she **trusted** in God, and as she **triumphed** at seeing her Savior face to face.

As I went through the process of caregiving, someone gave me a daily devotional that I faithfully read each morning. I could not put it down. When I finished, I searched for another that I could begin to read, but I could not find one with the power that I was searching for. It was at that time that I knew I had to write such a devotional so others could draw upon it for strength.

This book includes 24 devotionals. Each of the devotions includes a scripture reference, a brief inspirational or informational message, a continuing story, and reflection questions for use in journaling. It includes important information on spirituality, the importance of advanced planning, the supports available to caregivers, and the need for a strong relationship with God throughout the process.

While this book was meant to be read over a twenty-four days period, one devotion at a time, those that I have shared it with could not put it down. They finished it within several days. I encourage the reader to take the time to ponder the information and reflect on the goodness of God.

Acknowledgments

All glory and honor goes to God who provided the insight, inspiration and words for this book. I was happy to serve as the vessel to receive His messages.

Special acknowledgment to Susie H. Moody who lived the life for which this book honors.

I cannot begin to thank the many family members and friends who supported us during good times and bad, including her devoted sister, nieces, nephews, in-laws, friends and fellow Christians.

I acknowledge those who went on before her, including her loving and devoted husband, her brother, mother, aunts and uncles. I know they were all waiting for her as she entered the gates of Heaven.

Special thanks to her Pastor, and the many other clergy that respected her and supported her during her illness.

Thanks to all the clinicians and caregivers that tried to make her way easier.

Unless otherwise noted, the scripture passages are from the New King James Version (NKJV) of the Bible.

Foreword

I have learned to appreciate the wonderful memories as I grieve the loss of my grandmother. My sisters and I affectionately called her "MaMa". These memories have been a continuous source of comfort. Through reading this devotional, you will share in those memories and more importantly, be inspired in the journey of a caregiver as told by my mother. Please read and meditate on this devotional and follow the story of MaMa's transition—the introspective thoughts, moments of self-doubt, and the triumphant realizations.

I've always considered my mom a strong lady, but it was in this season of caregiving that I learned just how strong of a woman she is. I recall a conversation with my Dad in which I commented on her strength as she journeyed through the process of caring for my grandmother and he replied, "She's strong because she knows the source of her strength." In my nightly prayers, I prayed for this strength and even used my Facebook status feature as a vehicle for soliciting the prayers of the righteous. I prayed that as God watched over my grandmother and healed her in His own way, that He would continue to be the source of strength for my mother as she cared for her mother.

And so, dear caregiver, as you read this devotional, my prayer is the same for you as it was for my mom. I pray that you find this devotional a lamp unto your feet and a light unto your pathway (Psalm 119:105). I pray that whether caregiving is new for you, or it has been your calling for some length of time now, that you look to God for your refuge and strength. Believe that God will cover your loved one and He will keep you—the caregiver—in His keeping care.

Devotion 1

᭡

Jude 1:1-2

A Servant

Jude, a bondservant of Jesus Christ, and brother of James,
To those who are called, sanctified by God the Father,
and preserved in Jesus Christ: Mercy, peace, and love be multiplied to you.

Becoming a caregiver is an awesome responsibility and an automatic departure from the familiar. Routines must change, emotions become fluid, and uncertainty is a certainty. As caregivers, we must accept a change in lifestyle and accept the role of a servant. Servanthood is not for the meek at heart. Some people live their entire lives in servanthood to others. Others are forced into an unexpected circumstance of servanthood.

Regardless of the reason, we must remind ourselves often that we have been called for a special purpose. This calling means that we are covered by God the Father, and kept by Jesus Christ. We experience His abundance of mercy, peace, and love given to us and our loved ones.

As I write this story, it does not escape me that I am in the exact location that I was in a year ago. At that time, we traveled from our quiet home in the Maryland suburbs to the great playground of families in Orlando, Florida. We were not going for a relaxing vacation, but for a pilgrimage of service that my mother took every August. For at least the last forty years, she attended a Baptist convention that rotates to different cities throughout the country. She loved to take this trip every August for a week filled with spiritual classes, all-day preaching, and of course, a little Baptist drama.

On this occasion, my husband traveled to Orlando with us. He often travelled with his mother-in-law because, with the exception of our honeymoon or romantic getaways, mom was always there for every family trip. Even when dad was alive, mom would travel with us because he was not much for travelling. She enjoyed these opportunities to get away with the family she loved so dearly.

We hurried to get our luggage from the baggage claim, and as usual, mom had too many suitcases, and too many clothes. It is a tradition when coming to the convention. She had a bag for casual wear, a bag for dressy wear, shoes to match, and a bag just filled with convention materials for registration. She was in service as the registrar for the educational arm of the convention for many years and was getting ready for the nearly five thousand people that were expected to come and register.

For at least five of the seven days, she would spend her time serving others so that they could learn to rightly divide the Word of Christ. She was, as Jude, a servant of Jesus. She was one who was called, who was loved by God the Father and kept by Jesus Christ.

As much as she looked forward to fulfilling her responsibilities as a servant, she also enjoyed those breaks in the convention. She would go to dinner, shop, and then return to hear the Word of God from a different preacher each night, bringing a different message, with a different choir, but always the same climax of, "Jesus Got Up With All Power In His Hands."

Just as she liked to have her food seasoned with a lot of salt and pepper, she liked her religious activities seasoned as well. As much as she expressed disdain for the occasional shenanigans of the candidates running for office at the convention or questions on the budget report, she always looked forward to entering into a lively discussion with her sister, her constant companion. "Can you believe he said that?" she would ask. "What was she thinking?" They would talk until the late hours of the night, only to have to rise early in the morning to resume their duties.

Always a servant, always on duty, enjoying the spice, and enjoying life. She didn't realize that only a few months later she would be in need of help from a caregiver. She did not realize how drastically her life would change.

One year later, as I am writing this chapter, I have just returned from the convention that my mom loved so dearly and attended without fail. She was not able to attend, but I went because I knew this was important to her, and it edified my soul to see the people, eat the food, observe the spice, and hear some of the best preaching in the world. I knew I was called to the task of caregiving for this particular season. As surely as God had called me, He would keep me. He said so in His Word.

Journal Reflections

✥ When did your servanthood journey begin as a caregiver?

✥ Have you come to look upon this as a calling from God?

✥ Have you taken an opportunity to remind yourself that God will keep you in His abundance of mercy, peace, and love?

Devotion 2

☖

Jude 1:3

A Defender of the Faith

Beloved, while I was very diligent to write to you concerning our common salvation, I found it necessary to write to you exhorting you to contend earnestly for the faith which was once for all delivered to the saints.

During the process of caregiving, thoughts often cross our minds that should be fleeting; however, if we don't seek God's Word, they become lingering. We sometimes need that person who can just give us that "look" that means "straighten up and do what God would have us to do." It's not unnatural to need the kinds of reminders that Jude gives us in this Scripture because we are all human, and God often puts people in our paths to help us along the way. Jude tells us to stand up for our faith and defend it no matter the circumstance.

The convention was only one of many highlights in mom's Christian walk as she was always a servant in God's army, working to bring others to Christ in one way or another. She was a quiet, forceful power and the epitome of mercy, peace, and love. She was, as one minister put it when describing her, a defender of the faith, just like Jude. She loved as very few others have ever loved—unconditionally, always thinking of others. This always became evident on many of her shopping trips since she would spend her time shopping for others.

By July, she had finished purchasing most of her Christmas gifts. She would see something in a store and say, "Let me pick this up now because I know he or she will like this." She was genuinely concerned with making others happy.

As gentle and peaceful as she was, there was one subject that she did not take lightly, and that was following, teaching, and spreading the Word of the Lord. While she had her weaknesses—as we all do—faithfulness was not one of them. She knew to ask for forgiveness if she strayed and thought it her responsibility to help others from straying. In this vein, she also became known as the defender of the faith "feeling compelled to write and urge you to contend for the faith that was once for all entrusted to God's holy people" (Jude 1:3).

This faith tending was no joke to her. Although she attended college, she never completed it. In real terms and in life experiences, I felt as though she had earned a PhD. She possessed nearly every book written on the subject of Christianity, attended nearly every class offered on the subject (including Bible class at Howard University), taught nearly every class on the topic, served as a counselor for many ministers who sought her advice, and served as the Sunday school superintendent, director of Christian education, and deaconess at her church.

What was it about this small, meek, and soft-spoken lady that made her an authority that people would seek for her guidance? It's pretty simple now, in retrospect. God inhabited her spirit. Those around her knew that when they heard from her, they were hearing from God. They, including me as a little girl, knew that if she gave that look, it meant you were not stepping in the right direction. She became known for that look, and some coined it "Miss Susie's look." When you got the look, you knew to straighten up.

She would not stand for anyone, including herself, going against the faith that God had entrusted to her and to all of us. She was a constant reminder of God's love and mercy, and his firmness in the Word, all at the same time.

Journal Reflections

✧ Who is the person that you can turn to when you need a reminder of the path that we should take along this journey?

✧ When was the last time that you reached out to him or her? When will you plan to reach out to him or her again?

Devotion 3

∧∨

Jude 1:24

With great Joy

Now to Him who is able to keep you from stumbling,
And to present you faultless
Before the presence of His glory with exceeding joy,

God is a God of love and joy. During the caregiving process, we must learn to cherish happy moments and appreciate that God is in the middle of our joy. Some of the most joyous times that we have may be those times that we spend with our families as we unite with one another. Family is the first institution of God as He made His Family with Adam and Eve. He told them to go forth and multiply so that they could expand the family. We often hear the stories of family drama and difficulty, but far too few times do we celebrate the triumphs and the fun.

Even the Bible reminds us of family fun during wedding celebrations and feasts. It all belongs to God. When we are feeling down and heavy with burden, it is often helpful to think of the good times we shared together. If it is in God's will, those times will continue with the one for which we are giving care, and we should look forward to those times returning. We know that God is a healer and can do more than any physician can ever do. If it is not within His will, we know that God provides comfort and we will always have the precious memories that no one can take away.

Just after the convention, mom began another of her annual rituals and passages into the fall months, the annual shopping trip to New York. This was a trip that her mother started when she was younger and she continued it on for the rest of her life. I can remember traveling with my grandmother and mom to New York, staying at a hotel near 34th Street and having dinner at the *Automat* which was an upscale mix between a cafeteria and food vending machines. The *Automat* was much better because you simply put your money in the slots, opened up the little door and took out a complete hot meal. One window had food such as hot mashed potatoes and gravy; another had meatloaf; yet another had green beans and hot rolls. The most exciting part was the amazing dessert windows. I can remember putting all of the selections on a tray, selecting your table and dining as if you were at "Tavern on the Green." Although the *Automat* became extinct, the trips to New York continued. These trips to New York were always a joyful time filled with shopping, Broadway musicals, and family fun.

When my grandmother was no longer able to travel, my mother, aunt and her nieces continued the journey. As my children began to grow up, my husband and I continued the tradition with them. My middle daughter fell in love with the city and said, "One day, I will live here." She did, as a fashion design intern for a well known designer. This provided her with an opportunity of a lifetime, to live in New York while preparing for the infamous "New York Fashion Week".

These moments were special because they brought joy to us all as our adrenalin began to rise when we saw the bright lights of the city. We took a moment to enjoy all that God has made for us. We worked hard to save our money to enjoy these moments as they were more precious than any diamonds or rubies. They were times together with family, with fun, and with the abundance that God had provided to us; however so briefly, to know that He rules in all situations; even in fun.

Only weeks after mom's last trip to the convention in Orlando and her last trip to New York, she became ill and was not able to return to these places. This was the beginning of the caregiver journey, in a role I had never known before, even as a registered nurse that cared for many in the past.

Journal Reflections

✦ What are some of the fun events that you would like to remember and continue if God allows?

✦ If you can't continue them, how will you plan to remember them?

Devotion 4

1 Timothy 5:17a

Honor Your Elders

The elders who rule will be considered worthy of double honor

There are often groups in the community that can bring joy and honor to the lives of the elderly when they feel well and when they begin to feel under the weather. These groups actively engage in multiple activities such as senior outings, reading groups, scrapbooking or volunteering for household chores. The elderly and caregivers often, don't take advantage of these opportunities because of any number of reasons such as pride, fear of someone "getting into your business," thinking you have nothing in common with the groups, and the list goes on.

Take some time and seek out these groups for your parents or loved ones. Go with your loved one the first time if they are reluctant because they don't know anyone. Invite one of their friends to join them and let them know you will help pick up the first tab. These groups often provide an outlet for our loved ones and provide time for the caregiver. You can't always do it alone and you should not feel guilty because you can't. God puts people in your path that can help. Just reach out!

Mom was busy preparing for her next trip. She was traveling to Montreal with the Senior League Group. This group was special to her as they had monthly outings and one big trip in the fall. The trips were very reasonable as the church helped to defray some of the cost. This was as an outreach effort for seniors who frequently live on fixed incomes that are often devoured by the costs of prescription medications, utilities and other expenses. I began to think about how God sends people into your lives and how He has expectations of his Saints to care for and honor the elderly. Too often we think that means only saying "I'll pray for you." Prayer is obviously important and key for the elderly, but it is by no means the only thing that we can do. These Senior League opportunities were something that my mom and others looked forward to.

Several weeks in advance, we began going through our normal trip checklist and discussions. Mom would say, "Go to the bank and get me some money out of my account for the road."

"But mom" I would reply, "You have your ATM card now, you can just use that so you don't need a lot of cash."

"I know," she would answer, "You never know what might happen and you need cash. Also, I want you to run me to the store to pick up a couple of fall outfits."

"But mom, you have a closet full of clothes, some with the tags still on them."

"I know, but I need a few tops. Let's stop so I can get a few snacks for the road."

"But mom….." Always the same routine, always the same answers and as an obedient daughter, I did exactly as she instructed, after all, she was usually right and this was something I probably never told her enough. It was my duty and pleasure to honor her as the scripture instructs.

Running these errands were not hard for me, although time consuming. My mother moved in with us about three years prior. She had her own in-law suite in our basement. I simply had to run the items down the steps to her. It was such a blessing for me to have her living there. It was equally a blessing to have a husband willing to have his mother-in-law, a wife, and three daughters all living under one roof. I always told him how blessed he was. He would respond that he just wanted to find a TV in the house that wasn't on a "chick flick" or one of those reality shows.

As instructed, I began to run the errands. I went to the bank to get her cash, went to the store to get her snacks and then obediently went down the steps to give her the items before I left for a weekend trip to see my college daughter. I noticed that she was not feeling very well. A week out before she was to depart. I asked her if she would like to go to the emergency department. She had not felt well the week before and the doctor had prescribed some medication, it did not seem to help her. In fact, she was getting weaker. To my surprise, she said yes, she would go. At that point, I knew she was really not feeling well. Her normal response would have been "No, that's okay," especially when she knew I was about to go out of town. I wanted to get her to the emergency department to get treated quickly, get well and be ready to go on her trip with the group that meant so much to her.

Journal Reflections

❖ Have you explored groups in your church or community that may be able to provide a social outlet for your loved one?

❖ Give some consideration to the reason that may be stopping you from looking into this if you have not.

❖ If there are no groups operating in your area, is there an opportunity to bring this to the attention of your church, community center, mayor, congressperson or others? Others are likely to benefit from your actions.

Devotion 5

⚏

Isaiah 55:8-9

(New English Translation)

Only God Knows the Future

Indeed, my plans are not like your plans, and my deeds are not like your deeds, for just as the sky is higher than the earth, so my deeds are superior to your deeds and My plans superior to your plans.

Often time we think we have made the perfect plans, and; everything is under control. We plan our trip itineraries, work schedules, and caregiving schedules. We will give this medicine at this time and another at another time. We arrange for a nurse to come in at a certain time or to visit the hospital or nursing home at another time. All planned out and yet, our plans do not go as expected, and we have to change our course.

We can sometimes readily adjust, other times the very same change in plans causes us to be completely off kilter. We can't stop planning because we have to have some order to our lives. We have to seek God's guidance in our planning. Even when the plans change, we know that it is going just as God wanted it to go. We just weren't privy to the entire plan. He doesn't make mistakes, so we go where He leads us.

Stopped dead in her tracts! Just three weeks ago she was shopping in New York, going to plays, eating dinner, serving the Lord at her convention, providing wisdom to others, and now she is lying in the hospital bed weak, not eating, and discussing with me the need to call the trip organizer and cancel her attendance.

She planned so carefully, but this was not God's plan. Surely, this can't be, but it was. Oh well, missing one trip isn't the worst thing in the world. I know her sister, her travelling companion, will be concerned and wonder what she should do. My mom will be so disappointed, but at least she's in the hospital, can get well and get on her way.

We make all the necessary trip cancellation arrangements and concentrate on getting mom well. She was in the hospital for three days, and had become very weak. Every test had been done and there were some recommendations for outpatient tests that we would complete after discharge. She had lost a lot of weight over the past few weeks. We suspected that perhaps there was a cancer somewhere although none of the test had shown this to be the case.

We would follow-up on the needed test as an outpatient, but given her weakened condition, the recommendation was to transfer her to a rehabilitation center so she could regain her strength. Decision number one, should she be discharged to home or discharged to rehab? Mom never wanted to go into a nursing home or rehabilitation center. I could see she was visibly weak and believed that if she went to the rehab center for a few weeks she could get on her feet. We could then complete the outpatient workup that was recommended.

The doctor strongly recommended that she go and she asked her what she wanted to do. My mom looked at her and said, "Whatever my daughter thinks is best." She had come to rely on me as the trusted source. She knew I had my hands in God's hand, and that I loved her very much. She thought that I would do the right thing. This was an awesome responsibility.

I think I acted more on my medical knowledge than spiritual at the time, but prayed for God to intervene. For many weeks to come, I relied heavily on my knowledge of the medical system and the supports available, my knowledge of quality improvement techniques, and my knowledge of God. All in all I thought I had it under control.

She was discharged to the rehabilitation center, but would not eat, would not stand or cooperate with the physical therapist. She said that she was tired. We thought her refusal was because she did not want to do these things. As a result, we gave her all types of inspirational pep talks about what God can do, and keeping her faith. We later learned that she could not do these things because of a reaction to a medication that had weakened her muscles to the point that she had little control over them, including walking and swallowing. Within a few days, I authorized a transfer back to another hospital because she was not getting better, but getting worse.

Journal Reflections

✦ When was the last time you carefully made plans that didn't go as you expected?

✦ Did you consult God in the planning process?

✦ Are you flexible to His will if He takes you in a different direction?

Devotion 6

∿

Romans 12:3

Don't You Know Who I Am?

For by the grace given me I say to every one of you: Do not think of yourself more highly than you ought, but rather think of yourself with sober judgment, in accordance with the faith God has distributed to each of you.

Many times we think the journey is all about us. What did I do to deserve this? God, why aren't you listening to my prayer? Why do I have to do this, why not my sister or brother or someone else?" The answers may not be what you expect, and may not come at the moment that you ask the question. It may be weeks, years or eternity before you fully understand the answer. Just know that there is an answer, and with God, it's always the right answer. If we believe in Him, and let Him guide us through the challenges, we will always end up in the right place.

I soon found that working within the medical system is not always about what you know, who you know or the names that you drop. For even with my healthcare background as a registered nurse, there are just times in the system when the only one that can prevail is God. It was hard to imagine that my mom went through nearly every adverse medical event that you can think of including acquiring the worse pressure ulcer, a urinary tract infection associated with a catheter, an antibiotic resistant infection, a blood stream infection associated with having a catheter in her body, dehydration, reaction to her medication, and the list goes on.

How is it that this could be happening to me? Normally, I am a fairly quiet and humble person, not given to thinking more highly of myself than I ought, but this was my mother, and I didn't see the progress that I expected. I thought it was time to pull out the stops, and go down the road of "Don't these people know who I am? I am a healthcare professional working in the system. I was lost and perplexed about how this could be happening. I remember after one bout of "Don't you realize that just three weeks ago she was walking and packing and now she can do none of those things" and "Let me speak to the medical director," and, seeing that no matter how hard I tried, her story was not being adequately communicated from shift to shift, I became extremely frustrated. I felt completely helpless.

I sought the refuge of the chapel in the hospital. I tearfully asked God, "Why is this happening to me?" His answer came to me clearly.

"It's not happening to you. You are not lying in the hospital bed, she is."

I then asked "Why her? She has done nothing but good in her life, she has done nothing but serve you, she loves you more than anyone I know. She spent her life teaching others. Why her?" The answer was simple, although I did not hear it at the time. Only later did I understand the message from God as he told me, "She has one more lesson to teach you, and all the others that I will have her minister to."

It was many months later before I fully understood that even in her illness, she was teaching and ministering, and that it was not at all about me. I was to be an instrument for His messaging. She was to be the testimony for His goodness. Together we were to touch the lives of others going through this struggle of caregiving.

Journal Reflections

✧ Have you asked yourself, "What did I do to deserve this? God, why aren't you listening to my prayer?"

✧ Do you wonder "Why do I have to do this? Why doesn't this fall to my sister or brother or someone else?"

✧ Have you heard from God yet or considered the possible answers?

Devotion 7

Psalm 27

The Prayer

Often we must stop and pray to God about where we are, and where we are going. David prayed a special prayer that is very instructive as we go through the caregiving journey.

Psalm 27 was her favorite Psalm. Whenever anyone came to visit, and ask to read a scripture, she would request this Psalm. This Psalm is really a prayer from David. Some theologians say that there are two parts of the Psalm, the first being one of joy, encouragement, confidence, and praise during the good times.

Commentators often note that the second part of the scripture was written during a time when David was seeking help, when times were difficult.

God has led me to believe there is indeed a third part. I believe we see the transition from first, good times and praise, to secondly, the request for help during difficult times, and finally to a promise from God.

I believe that the promise is clearly stated, distinct from the other two parts. In the third part, we have the promise that if we are of good courage, and wait on the Lord, He will strengthen us. He will strengthen us beyond all imagination. He will strengthen us beyond anything we could ever wish for or desire.

It is this promise that sustained mom for all that was to follow. It was this promise that carried me and my family through the tough days ahead.

Psalm 27

1 *The LORD is my light and my salvation;*
    Whom shall I fear?
    The LORD is the strength of my life;
    Of whom shall I be afraid?
2 *When the wicked came against me*
    To eat up my flesh,
    My enemies and foes,
    They stumbled and fell.
3 *Though an army may encamp against me,*
    My heart shall not fear;
    Though war may rise against me,
    In this I will be confident.

4 *One thing I have desired of the LORD,*
    That will I seek:
    That I may dwell in the house of the LORD
    All the days of my life,
    To behold the beauty of the LORD,
    And to inquire in His temple.
5 *For in the time of trouble*
    He shall hide me in His pavilion;
    In the secret place of His tabernacle
    He shall hide me;
    He shall set me high upon a rock.

6 *And now my head shall be lifted up above my enemies all around me;*
    Therefore I will offer sacrifices of joy in His tabernacle;
    I will sing, yes, I will sing praises to the LORD.

7 *Hear, O LORD, when I cry with my voice!*
    Have mercy also upon me, and answer me.
8 *When You said, "Seek My face,"*
    My heart said to You, "Your face, LORD, I will seek."
9 *Do not hide Your face from me;*
    Do not turn Your servant away in anger;
    You have been my help;
    Do not leave me nor forsake me,
    O God of my salvation.
10 *When my father and my mother forsake me,*
    Then the LORD will take care of me.

¹¹ *Teach me Your way, O LORD,*
  And lead me in a smooth path, because of my enemies.
¹² *Do not deliver me to the will of my adversaries;*
  For false witnesses have risen against me,
  And such as breathe out violence.
¹³ *I would have lost heart, unless I had believed*
  That I would see the goodness of the LORD
  In the land of the living.

¹⁴ *Wait on the LORD;*
  Be of good courage,
  And He shall strengthen your heart;
  Wait, I say, on the LORD!

Journal Reflections

✦ Write the first few words of each of the three phases of the prayer. Do you recognize the promise from God?

✦ Write down verses that especially speak to you. We will explore all of these verses over the next several pages of the devotional.

Devotion 8

✛

Psalm 27:1(a)

Fearful but not Afraid

The LORD *is* my light and my salvation; Whom shall I fear?

We often find ourselves in situations that may frighten us. We may have fear because we have observed bad outcomes in others or simply a lack of faith in this instance. Regardless of the situation, we can always draw upon the one thing that is certain.

If we have accepted the Lord as our personal Savior, He has made promises to be with us, lead us, guide us and provide a home in heaven above all other homes we may find ourselves in on earth. This knowledge and assurance can help us face those fearful times without being afraid.

As mom moved from the hospital back to a different nursing home for rehabilitation, I believe that she was fearful that she would never come home. She stated to me that she wondered why I was sending her to this place as "People never come home from there." While she never showed any real signs of fear, and never once to this day shed any tears that I could see, I believe she was fearful of this place where she would reside for the next several weeks.

Having been through the journey of nursing homes with both my grandmother and father, and working in the healthcare profession, I began to pull out my resources to review the facility to which she would be transported. I reviewed every website, and there are many that rate the quality of care. I read every brochure, spoke with others, and drew upon my experience in my church where I am often called upon to visit parishioners in nursing homes.

All of this research was helpful when looking at the percentage of times the nursing home had people develop bed sores or pressure ulcers. I reviewed how they ranked with staffing and managing pain in the residents. I also reviewed whether they had twenty-four hour visitation for family members, how many times we could expect the doctor to visit, did they have a wound care specialist, and the quality of the physical therapy services. I asked the residents what they thought of the food and I observed for cleanliness.

I then thought of things such as convenience. Often people think of convenience first, but I have come to learn that what may have been most convenient for me was not necessarily the best for mom. Even if it meant I had to drive a little further, take the bus a little longer, or walk an extra mile, it was better to be in a reputable facility.

Working closely with the social worker at the hospital, we decided on a place that would meet our needs, help mom to recover, and get her back home as quickly as possible. That was my plan. I had to believe this because I knew she didn't want to be in this facility.

She entrusted decisions regarding the course of her care to me, her only child. She devoted her life to taking care of me, and now I must do likewise as the Bible clearly directed me in 1 Timothy 5:8, "But if anyone does not provide for his relatives, and especially for members of his household, he has denied the faith and is worse than an unbeliever." I knew that, in this instance, it meant making the hard choice of sending her to a place that I thought could help her even if she were fearful.

The one thing that was evident was that even if she was fearful of the particular situation, she was not afraid of any ultimate outcome. If she never had the opportunity to come back to her physical home, she was confident and assured of her salvation.

She knew that Jesus was the light of her life, and no matter where she was, He would be there with her. She knew that if she called upon Him, He would be there whether the nurse, medical assistance, or any of her family members heard her. Jesus was her salvation. She had no fear of her ultimate home, only this temporary new home.

Journal Reflections

✤ When were you last afraid?

✤ What was your first reaction?

✤ How did you reassure yourself?

✤ Are you confident in your salvation and your ultimate home above all other homes?

Devotion 9

∆∇

Psalm 27:1(b)

You Need Your Strength

The LORD *is* the strength of my life; Of whom shall I be afraid?

Many times we think our strength comes only from food that we eat. We worry about meal preparations, and take the time to plan out our menus for the week, stop by the grocery store, and spend time going up and down the aisles. We often worry because our loved one is not eating as they should or that we are spending so much time taking care of them that we are not preparing the meals that we should for our own family. We are concerned about that favorite dish that our returning college student looks forward to or that special Sunday meal that our spouse desires.

How will we get it all done, and still have time to provide the care that we need to for our loved one. While it's all very important, and we can't forget about our family, we must take time to feed on God's Word for it is through his Word that we find the strength, and supernatural ability to take care of all the other needs that our families and loved ones have. It is His Word that gives us strength. Our strength comes from the Lord.

"You need to eat so you can keep up your strength." I must have said this about a hundred times during mom's recovery. As soon as her sister came in she would repeat the same words. Later her nurses and her doctors would recite the same words. She would look at us, nod her head in agreement, and not eat one more thing. Mom was never a very big eater. She was a very picky eater, not wanting to venture too far away from familiar foods.

We all loved to go to dinner with her because you could always count on the fact that she would share whatever she had on her plate. She would eat a few spoonfuls here and a few there. Her favorite food was fried shrimp. She would eat one or two shrimp, and then begin to dole the food out to everyone else's plate, sometimes without even asking if they wanted it. You would suddenly find a few shrimp on your plate with her saying "Here take these, I have too many." We had all become accustomed to her eating habits.

But, even though she didn't eat a lot, she ate enough to sustain her. I can recall worrying that she would not be able to find enough to keep her going as we prepared for a ten day trip to Europe. This was a quickly planned trip that came about after a pilgrimage to the Holy Land fell through because of a travel advisory. We saved for nearly two years to go to the Holy Land, and now all bets were off. Our money was refunded. Within days, I booked a trip to Europe with stops in London, Paris and Rome.

Little did I know at the time that God, yet again, was guiding our path. As mom had already made one trip to the Holy Land, she had never visited these well known tourist stops. The two of us launched off with a tour group for which we had no familiarity. As we walked in the Apostle Paul's footsteps in Rome, looked upon the Apostle Peter's burial site, and cruised down the Seine in Paris, she remarked that it was one of the highlights of her life and she never forgot those precious moments.

My biggest fear in the quick planning process was that she would not find any food that she liked in those foreign lands, and that she would lose her strength during the travels. She never seemed concerned, which was very curious to me. It is clear that mom's strength never came from the food that she ate.

While we worried about her eating, she did not. Her strength came from the Lord, and from the food that can sustain you eternally, His Holy Word. We didn't have to worry about what restaurant to seek out to find her food. She traveled with her Bible; her sustenance was in her purse everywhere she went. To the ends of the earth, His Word will always strengthen and sustain us.

Journal Reflections

✦ Think of your favorite food to eat. How many times have you had it in the last month?

✦ Think of the spiritual food that we eat as we read His Word. How many times have you sat with your Bible in the last month, and partaken of the blessings that God has prepared for you?

Devotion 10

∧∨

Psalm 27:2

The Flesh is Weak

When the wicked came against me; To eat up my flesh,
My enemies and foes, They stumbled and fell.

Sometimes we find ourselves in what appears to be hopeless situations. The doctors have given a bad report or the hard work that we put in doesn't seem to be making much of a difference. Our loved one doesn't seem to be doing what they need to get well. We just don't understand it when they say "I can't." What do you mean "You can't?"

What we should remember is the very moment when they can't and we can't, is when God is at His greatest. He CAN do all things. We have to learn to trust in His all knowing power, and know that he will do the things that we can't do alone. He will take care of all enemies, foes, diseases and challenges. He sent doctors and nurses and therapist to help us, but we all have to give it over to Him and He CAN.

"She has a stage four pressure ulcer," The doctor said in a matter of fact manner. "There are only four stages," I state. "So this is about as bad as it can get?" I knew that stage four meant that the full thickness of her skin was lost with extensive destruction of her flesh including damage to muscle, and bone. As noted in Psalm 27:2, the enemies had come to eat her flesh. This kind of damage to the flesh doesn't happen overnight, but it can happen quickly in a small frail elderly woman such as mom.

It usually begins with a little reddening of the skin. This reddening began during day two of her three day hospital stay. It is called a hospital acquired pressure ulcer, and is considered a preventable event, but here it was. When she was transferred to the nursing home, the pressure ulcer began to worsen. The nursing home staff shook their heads and said, "Those hospitals just don't do the right thing to prevent this." When she was transferred back to the hospital, the hospital staff shook their heads and said, "Those nursing homes just don't know what to do to prevent this." I shook my head and said, "This should never have happened on my watch. How can this be?" But, here it was, a stage four pressure ulcer.

The key to healing, in this situation, is proper nutrition with a goal of getting more protein into her, a good mattress, frequent turning, dressing changes, and a will to not let the enemy have victory when coming to eat of the flesh. I can't remember the number of times I was told that this pressure ulcer would not heal; it was too deep, she was too sick, only surgery could fix it. She was not a candidate for surgery, and the list goes on.

The enemy came against her flesh many times. She was in pain on many occasions because of the pressure ulcer. It began to dominate her course of treatment because she could not sit up in a chair for a long time, they could not do aggressive physical therapy because of it. It became frustrating for me because I knew that mom needed to eat to fight this thing off, but she would not. I didn't understand why she would not eat until she told me one day, "It's not that I don't want to eat, I just can't."

I still don't fully understand the "I just can't." I suppose someday I will when someone puts a tray of food in front of me filled with my favorite things and I just can't. I hope that if that day comes, I handle it with the grace that she did. She didn't yell at anyone, she didn't tell people to "Just leave me alone." She just said, "I can't."

We discussed the placement of a permanent feeding tube for nourishment and protein to heal her flesh. I thought her answer would be a resounding "NO."

It was not, she agreed with no argument. We had the tube placed during a one day outpatient surgery. She began to get her protein. She received extensive therapy for her pressure ulcer, and over the course of months, the pressure ulcer, that no one thought would heal, did indeed heal. The site that was down to the bone began to fill in with what is call granulation tissue.

Folks thought it was a miracle, and in some respects, it was. It was a demonstration that although the wicked will come against us to eat up our flesh, they can be made to stumble and fall, and we can be made whole by the power of the Holy Spirit.

Journal Reflections

✦ Has your loved one refused to do something that you think they should do?

✦ What were your thoughts at that time?

✦ How did you handle your feelings? Remember that God can do exceedingly great things even when we as humans can't.

Devotion 11

✳

Psalm 27:3

Confidence through the Battle

Though an army may encamp against me, My heart shall not fear;
Though war may rise against me, In this I *will be* confident.

Sometimes it feels as though there is no escape from our troubles. The
enemy surrounds us on every front. The enemy may be our lack of time,
our bills, our lack of understanding in why healing is not occurring,
and our fear of what lies ahead. Regardless of the enemy, we must be
confident in whose we are. When our world begins to suffocate us, we
must try to remain steadfast and confident in our ministry and calling,
helping others through the battle.

Mom suffered through four hospital stays including a seven day stay in the
ICU; three months of a nursing home rehabilitation stay; sixteen needle
sticks at one time to get an intravenous line started; multiple tests, x-rays
and procedures; catheters placed here and there; specialists upon specialists
with second, third and forth opinions. Surely, it must have felt as if an army
was on the attack.

This once strong woman was now in the midst of everything she
had spent her wholelife teaching about, telling others about, and that
was having strength and keeping the faith even when the army was
surrounding her.

She was always a proud and private woman. She didn't "tell her business" to many. While she had some dear friends, she was not one to need a lot of people around. She was always confident and independent. She also instilled that in me. I in turn, instilled that independence in my three daughters.

She would never want to be seen without her matching pant or skirt suit, earrings, hair piece, a little light lipstick, and her glasses. Yet, here she lay in bed with none of those things. She was still confident, still believing and still teaching and defending the faith.

Although she didn't want visitors initially, she soon knew that she still had a calling from God, even as she lay in her bed. My husband and I are both Deacons at our church. We have been for several years. In the Baptist church, Deacons are called upon to assist the Pastor in assuring the spiritual well being of the Church. Our tasks are many, but making disciples of men and caring for the sheep that God has provided in the congregation is primary.

Caring for the sheep or the sheepfold, as we call them, means visiting when they are sick. We were in the process of working with our fellow Deacons to train new Deacons. They are called Deacons-in-Training or DITs.

As a part of the practicum, the DITs must go out to the sheepfold in the hospital and nursing home. They share the scriptures, pray, and visit for a short while on behalf of the Church and the Pastor. We were assigned two DITs to train in this area. We thought of several people we might have them go and visit, none of which had been my mom, understanding her need for privacy and not wanting visitors.

After a few visits had fallen through, I asked mom if she would mind if we brought the DITs to see her as they needed to get their training before the next classroom session. I told her that they would pray for her. They would minister to her to make her feel better. In her weakened state, I thought she would reply no, but again, never ceasing to amaze me, her reply was "Sure. I can help train them."

While I said that the DITs will come to minister to her, what she heard was she would help them. She could not let an opportunity pass by to do God's work, even in the condition she was in.

As the time approached for them to come, she quickly gave me instructions such as, "Give me that hairpiece over there, hand me my glasses, and pull me up in the bed." She sat proudly and confidently waiting their arrival. She was confident in the assurance that even though the enemy sat in camp around her, she still knew who was in control. She was willing to share this great news with those in training. They came, read the scriptures, visited, and prayed. God's presence filled the hospital room. The anointing was truly felt by all.

When they left, I asked her, "How did they do?" She smiled proudly, as if she had just completed teaching a full semester and said, "They did fine, just fine. I told them I would see them at ordination."

Journal Reflections

✦ What are the special gift that your love one possesses?

✦ What special gifts do you possess?

✦ How can you use those gifts to help someone else?

✦ How can you demonstrate your confidence that God will see you through even though you may feel that you are at your lowest point?

Devotion 12

∿

Psalm 27:4(a)

Asking God for the things you Desire

One *thing* I have desired of the LORD, That will I seek:

What is the one thing you desire today? We often spend time thinking about the past, which is now over, and the future, which is not promised. God has placed us in this season of caregiving for the present, and he will answer our prayers if we only ask Him. Just think of today and this moment.

What is the one thing that you desire? Our scripture goes on to tell us that David desired to dwell in the house of the Lord, and we can all be blessed by, and desire that one thing. We will discuss David's desire in a later devotion, but what is the one thing you desire today? Is it a little nap because you have been busy balancing caregiving with work, church and family?

Is the one thing you desire today a pain free day for your loved one because they have gone through so much pain the past few days? Is the one thing an opportunity to go out to dinner with your spouse because you haven't had an evening out in a while? The one thing might be that you maintain your own health during the process.

There may be many one things that you can think of for the day. The one thought that is important is that God can make those one things happen if we believe, trust, and ask Him. God tells us that we have not because we ask not. Matthew 7:7-8 tells us "Ask, and it shall be given you; seek, and ye shall find; knock, and it shall be opened unto you: For every one that ask will receive; and he that seek will find; and to him that knock, it shall be opened."

One thing that mom really wanted was to come home. After months of hospitals and nursing homes, she had enough. She likely didn't think she would come home as she had planted in her mind that "People don't leave those places," but she never gave up hope.

After so many life and death moments and transfers, I wasn't sure that I would be able to care for her at home. I had a full time job, a family, and loads of responsibilities at church. She needed total care around the clock.

Several occurrences began to reveal God's plan for my mom. First, the doctors told me for about the fifth time that there was nothing else they could do for her. She was not thriving. During the previous times, I did not agree with them. I told them we wanted aggressive therapy. God had not yet told me that he wanted me to do anything else but aggressive therapy. My mom had not told me anything differently either.

This time; however, I felt that it was in the will of God to listen to the doctors and decide on the next steps. They recommended that I consider Hospice care. They noted that I could receive this care even while she was in the nursing home.

That night, my husband and I lay in the bed discussing mom's care as we had on many other nights. He said that he thought it would be better if mom came home. I had thought this on several occasions, but wondered how the family would feel. It was such a blessing to hear this son-in-law say "Bring mom home."

I'm sure it's more than he had ever signed up for in the "better or worse" department, but he was there, fully supportive. I'll even help he said, I just can't clean up any bodily fluids (something he didn't like to do very much even for our own kids) but I can do anything else.

I began to wonder, how I can make this *one thing* that was so important happen. The next day I had a discussion with the hospice nurse about giving care at home rather than the nursing home, I spoke with the doctor about what would be involved with discharge.

I told my mom that the doctors didn't think they could do very much more for her there until she got stronger. I asked her if she would like to seek more opinions or would she prefer to come home. Her face lit up, and without a word of hesitation she said, "Come home." I knew that if I made one step God would take care of the rest.

I know that coming home is not always the best answer for everyone. Some people will need the support of the nursing home. When this is the case, the caregiver should not feel guilty about that decision. For mom, and this moment, God was about to grant her desire. She was discharged to home three days later.

Journal Reflections

✛ What is your one desire of God for today?

✛ Take this opportunity to go to Him in prayer. Ask of Him your desire-- believing, as in Matthew 7: 7-8, that if you ask, you will receive.

Devotion 13

∿

Psalm 27:5(a)

Making Provisions in Caregiving

For in the time of trouble, He shall hide me in His pavilion;

Much of the help that we need is readily awaiting us when we respond "Yes" to the offers of help that are available. Much of this help is available regardless of income. We often need only talk to someone, and investigate the resources. These resources often go untapped because we may be looking for God to answer our prayers in different ways. We can't out guess God. He has promised to hide us in His pavilion or protect us. Be open, and willing to getting your protection in whatever form He chooses to send it.

It is always amazing to see how God works. You can never predict how His goodness will be granted. You can only know with assurance that it will. Once we made the decision to bring mom home, things began to fall into place without a hitch. Many thought it was because I was a nurse that everything began to work out, but I knew it was God.

While being a nurse may have allayed a little of my anxiety, I had never experienced this type of transition in care from nursing home to home. My father transitioned from the hospital to a nursing home, but he passed away in the nursing home. It had been many years since I had any experience with home care, and even then it was as a student. I learned as I went along, and found out a few things I wished I had known earlier.

First, there was the choice between home care and hospice care. In both instances, you receive the support of qualified medical professionals in your home, but the purposes are different. Usually, in home care, you have nurses, aides, and therapist that come in to help you get well and back on your feet. The sessions may be intense at the beginning with physical therapy, occupational therapy, speech therapy, nursing care, and other services. As you get better, the services decrease until you can handle yourself or with the assistance of your family. Many families are now choosing long term home health care rather than in center nursing home care. This is an option that is growing in popularity.

Hospice care, on the other hand, assists you as you transition through the final stages of life. Visits become more frequent versus less at the end of Hospice. The doctor suggested that I explore hospice care. I was familiar with the hospice benefit for cancer care, but mom didn't have cancer. I asked, "Will she qualify for that type of care? After all, mom is going to come home and get better, not come home and die," I retorted.

After speaking with the hospice representative, speaking with God and other family members, I agreed to the hospice care. Mom was in pain, she didn't want to be in the nursing home, and she was not thriving. She was in fact near death if nothing changed. The hospice representative noted that no one knows exactly when she would pass away. If she got better, we could always stop and convert to home care. In the mean time, they provided special services that could make her days at home more comfortable.

Within a day, the hospital bed showed up at the house, a wheel chair, a toilet seat, and other equipment that would be necessary to help me manage her at home. The one issue that appeared to cause concern was that she had a permanent feeding tube. They noted that feeding tubes always seemed to complicate things.

Artificial feedings may stand in the way of the natural progression of a person's transition. They asked if I planned to continue it. I replied, "Yes." After all, she came home with the stage four pressure ulcer (which ultimately healed) and she needed to get the protein in her to help it heal. Even if she was not going to live a long life, there was no reason for her to have to live in pain with this huge wound covering most of her buttocks area. Healing this wound, in my opinion, was a comfort measure, not aggressive therapy.

God opened up a window, and I was able to get all the supplies I needed to care for her feeding tube and the nutritional supplements that she was to be fed. Soon after that, the doorbell rang. I went to the door. It was the pharmacy delivering all of the medications I would need to keep her comfortable.

A few minutes later, the telephone rang. It was the chaplain from the hospice making arrangements to come and pray with mom and me. Later the next day, the social worker called, then the volunteers came. My aunt and her family soon came bringing in water, tissues and supplies.

It was apparent that "*in the time of trouble, He shall hide me in His pavilion*" (*Psalm 27:5*). While we were not physically in His temple, the temple is not a building. The church is the people, all of the people that he sent to help her–people from all walks of life that surrounded us, and hid us safely from the isolation and despair.

Journal Reflections

❖ Can you think of a time when God blessed you in a way that you didn't expect?

❖ How did you feel at that moment when you realized that you had received this unexpected blessing?

❖ How can you turn that surprise and amazement into an expectation that God will always help you in His own way and own time? This my friend is called TRUST.

Devotion 14

⋀⋁

Psalm 27:5(b)
Living the High Life

In the secret place of His tabernacle He shall hide me;
He shall set me high upon a rock.

As caregivers, we find that there are often things that we need or that our loved one needs that insurance will not cover. We aren't always sure of whether we can afford these "luxuries" because we can barely take care of the necessities. We should not put God in a box, thinking we can only do what is in our meager means. God can do more than we ever could. He blesses us in abundance.

Take a chance. Look into assistance that you need. Perhaps you can cover it out of pocket or from your loved one's financial nest egg. Otherwise, take a look at community resources. Ask for help from church members, volunteers, state agencies, and others. Many states now have programs that allow you to care for your loved one in the home and still receive assistance.

Another source of help comes through "Long Term Care Insurance." If your loved one doesn't have it already, it may or may not be worth the investment at this point, although you can investigate it. Perhaps now is the time to look into coverage for yourself, your spouse, or make a suggestion to other loved ones. Remember we all must cross this path some day.

Take the opportunity to learn from what your loved one is going through to plan for your own period of transition. I always remember the wisdom of my husband's grandmother, a domestic worker with meager means. Regardless how little the wage she was paid for the day, she managed to save some for a rainy day.

Our scripture for this devotion tells us we will be placed high upon a rock. Usually, when we hear the term "living the high life," we think of the lifestyles of the rich and the famous. We begin to think of riding around in limousines, draping furs around our shoulders, and toasting a glass of champagne.

When your life is turned upside down by illness and chronic conditions, the high life or sitting high upon a rock as our scripture suggests, can take on a whole new meaning. It can be a high point just to be able to walk to the bathroom without assistance, being able to turn yourself in the bed from one side to the other, getting a glass of water without someone helping you, or even having someone there to help you if you need a sip of water.

Living the high life for mom began to mean these very things. Both my husband and I worked fulltime jobs (and needed to continue with children in college). Mom required full time care. We wanted her home with us so we had to quickly come up with a plan to help her live the high life of just being able to get through her activities of daily living.

Yet again, a miracle happened when we explored the possibility of getting a home aide to come in five days a week while I was working. The miracle was not so much in getting the aide, but in who God sent as the aide. We were blessed to get a hard working Christian woman who was very compatible with mom.

This wonderful union happened with the very first aide we brought in, which is not always the case. Sometimes you have to work with several aides to find the right person. It is important to feel comfortable with the person in your home when you are not there.

I shopped around to find someone that was reasonably priced because the price does vary from agency to agency. This level of care is usually not covered by regular health insurance. My only regret is that I had not done this sooner, even when she was well. It would have made a great deal of sense to have this aide come in once or twice a month when mom was well because they can take you out for doctors visits or the mall, help with light cleaning, help prepare meals, and all types of activities. It would have given her a sense of independence because she didn't want to always infringe upon our time to do such errands (although I smile because I think we spent our fair share of time in the malls and going to dinner).

This seemed to be a luxury that only the rich could afford or one that mom would not want because of her private nature. In retrospect, it was affordable, and something that mom would have adjusted to quickly.

But, now we had our angel of an aide. She was there faithfully every day. She helped with bathing, changing bed linens, and washing. She hummed a tune every morning as she helped with the bath. She was respectful of our home, and respectful of my mom. I thank God every day for her presence. I know He handpicked her for us. He sits us upon a "high rock" and lets us live the "high life" of just daily living.

Journal Reflections

✢ Have you put God in a little box, ruling out possibilities that might help you without even exploring them?

✢ What plans have you made for your own golden years?

Devotion 15

Psalm 27:6(a)

Lifting Up Your Loved One

And now my head shall be lifted up above my enemies all around me;

It is important for our loved ones to know they are loved, and for them to be able to express their love in their own way. Even if your loved one was not always there for you or you had a challenging past with them, don't pass up this opportunity to forgive, let go, and tell them you love them. We love because God expects us to love. Don't spend the rest of your life wishing that you had.

I was blessed to have had a wonderful relationship with my mom all of my life. Yet, even with that, I know there were times when more love could have been expressed.

How many times have you heard "I wish I would have said…." or "I wish I would have told them…" Well stop wishing and do it. We often learn more about people at their memorial service than we did when they were alive. We say such wonderful things about them once they are not around to hear it. None of us know when we will come to the end of our journey, so we should treat each day as if it were our last.

Mom was a very quiet person. She was not one to show a great deal of emotion. She was the oldest of three children. Quite often she took on the posture of the strong matriarch who remained cool, calm, and in control. Even though she was not very expressive or "touchy-feely," you always knew she loved you by her actions. She never had to say a word because she just exuded love.

During her illness, she remained cool and calm, occasionally smiling and saying things a little out of character such as "Just hold my hand." or "Just hug me." Sometimes I would ask how she was doing and she would reply, "Better now that I see you." We were always sure to get a smile when her grandchildren and nephews came down to see her. She could be refusing to do something that I just asked her to do, or pushing away some medicine she was to take, and then suddenly in another minute, when the grandchildren entered the room, she let out the loudest, "Hello sweetheart!"

We were fortunate to celebrate two special occasions with mom right after her return home, her birthday, and Mother's day. While we took the opportunity daily to say what we wanted, these were special days. Although she was in the bed, we brought the party to her. We sat with her in her room eating cake and ice cream. We had big balloons all around. The kids laughed and played, the music was playing. Someone walking in would question whether this was a sick room.

It wasn't a sick room to us, it was a healing room. These days would bring a smile to her face, even if she didn't say very much. We read our tributes to her through our cards. We said our words of love to her. These are cherished memories that we will always have, and we are glad that God provided us the opportunity to say it when she was alive rather than when she is gone.

Journal Reflections

❖ Have you taken the opportunity to express your love to someone close to you?

❖ Is there someone you need to forgive and contact that you have not in a while? Let go and let God move in your life. We may not have this chance again.

Devotion 16

◢◥

Psalm 27:6(b)
Count it all Joy

Therefore I will offer sacrifices of joy in His tabernacle;
I will sing, yes, I will sing praises to the LORD.

We should always seek ways to stay connected to God, even during our caregiving. We can always turn on a radio or television service to hear an inspirational Word. God has also moved through technology so that we have even more options for staying connected.

You may need to identify a church that has live streaming webcasts, or explore tuning into Bible study by way of a conference call line. Many websites have daily devotionals. Perhaps there is a Bible study in a neighborhood church closer to you than your home church.

Lamentations 3: 22-24 reminds us that every morning the Lord has NEW mercies. Search for new ways to stay connected to Him even though your routine may be changing.

Joy? You call this Joy? Making sure the position is changed every two hours, needing two people to help get her out of bed, making sure she doesn't fall, struggling to juggle schedules, coordinating visits with the doctors and other care providers, hearing "Why were you gone so long?" when in reality it was only a few minutes. Joy?

The answer is yes. Joy is what dwells within you, not what happens to you. The arrows will keep coming, the peaks and the valleys won't go away, but that Joy that God gives is everlasting. It's the Joy of having the privilege to serve. To be God's angel on earth. It could be you lying in the bed, but instead, you have the honor of caring for one of God's children. He is with you every step of the way.

I couldn't help but praise Him when I looked at her. With all of her pain and suffering, she still praised Him. My church's prayer ministry stopped by to see my mom one Saturday afternoon. Some of them knew her, but others did not because she belonged to another church.

There were about seven people. As one of the members entered the bedroom, he exclaimed, I feel the spirit in this place. They knew right away that God had met them there, and He was waiting for them to lift Him up. They began to sing, pray, and say a few words. Mom sang along with them. She was no stranger to His spirit.

I sang as loud as anyone because I was so thankful to God for His goodness and for these people that He sent to lift Him up. Even in the darkest moments, I will sing praises to God. The opportunities to sing His praises may be different than those that existed before we became caregivers.

We may not be able to go to church as often as we use to, we may not be able to make it to choir rehearsal or teacher's meeting. We can be creative and be open to doing things differently for this is only a season and God has equipped us for this season.

Journal Reflections

❖ How are you staying connected to God as you go about your caregiving duties?

❖ What new ideas can you think of to maintain the joy that dwells within?

Devotion 17

$\bigwedge$

Psalm 27:7

How will I know God's Will?

Hear, O LORD, *when* I cry with my voice! Have mercy
also upon me, and answer me.

*When God answers your prayer, as He always does, you must be ready
for His response. It may not be what you wanted when you wanted it,
but He will answer your cry. We must be vigilant, steadfast, stay in His
will, and He will make the answer clear to us. God is faithful in His
Word and He is faithful to those that serve Him.*

Frequently during the caregiving process, I found myself asking God what
He would have me do in a particular situation. It was not always clear to
me what steps I should take next or what mom would want done. The nurse
would often remind me that at some point I needed to make a decision about
this feeding tube that was interrupting the natural course of events.

How will I know when it's right to discontinue these feedings? How will
I know when it's right to let nature take its course? How long should I let her
suffer? Was I doing this thinking she could get well or to keep her around so
we could have her with us as long as we wanted?

I knew that these answers did not lie within in me, but within God. My
only action was to say as David said, "Hear, O LORD, *when* I cry with my
voice! Have mercy also upon me, and answer me" (Psalm 27:7). Please Lord;
provide the answers that I seek.

Perhaps it would be better for her and everyone if he took her home now. Perhaps it would be better if he kept her here five more years and she could see her great-grandchildren. Perhaps, perhaps, perhaps. The only answer for me was being obedient to His will. Whatever you want me to do, I will do. If it's turn every two hours, I will do it. If it's continuing the feedings, I will do it. If it's preparing the family for her death, then I will do it. I will do whatever you would have me do. Just please give me the answer.

Mom's condition continued to deteriorate, and I continued to seek His will, and wondered how I would know what His answer was. Saturday was my birthday, and I had a long standing tradition of attending the Smooth Jazz festival on my birthday. This was a daylong event so I made special arrangements to have the home aide come in for the day so that I could go to the concert.

Before going, I went to conduct my morning routine of starting mom's tube feeding, giving her medications, and turning her. I went in the room, and said, "Hello mom, it's my Birthday and I'm going to the jazz festival." She smiled, as she knew the tradition well.

While mom never was big on dancing, concerts or parties, she knew I picked this up from my father who never let the music start without him moving on to the dance floor. I checked her to make sure she was dry as several weeks ago she had pulled out the urinary catheter on her own. She handed it to the nurse telling her she didn't need it anymore, although she was incontinent with a wound. It was one of the incidences that you couldn't help but chuckle about, although it wasn't really what you would have desired. We went with her wishes as she was the boss in this case.

I began to flush her tube, and it looked as if there were coffee grounds in the tube. I knew this was a sign of dried blood. I flushed the tube, and it was still open. I thought for a minute that I should hold the feeding, but I decided I should go ahead and give it as I would be away for a while at the concert and did not want her to be hungry. I began to hang the feeding bag, and she said, "I don't want it."

She had never told me that she didn't want a tube feeding before because it was pretty effortless for her.

I said, "Mom are you sure?"

She said, "Yes."

Given the coffee ground substance in the tube earlier, I thought that it was probably a good idea to hold the feeding because she could still have some bleeding in her stomach. It would probably be better to wait and see what was going on. I flushed the tube some more with water. I observed for awhile and went on my way.

Later that evening after my return, I went to relieve the home aide, and start the medication and feeding routine. The nurse said that my mom was particularly quiet that day. I went in to say hello, talk about the festival, and give the medications. I prepared the feeding and began to hang it. She looked at me, and said, "I don't want it."

I said, "Mom you haven't had anything to eat all day." She had long ago stopped eating anything by mouth. I reached to connect the feeding, despite her expressed desire. She forcefully removed my hand with such strength that it startled me because I didn't know she had that much strength left.

"I don't want it," she said looking me directly in the eye. It was at that moment that I knew God had provided the answer that I was seeking. My question had been "How will I know when to decide?" The answer was that the decision was not up to me; it was between her and God, and they had made the decision.

Journal Reflections

✦ Are you listening for God's answer to your cries?

✦ Do you believe that He hears your request? God is a God of love and will never fail.

Devotion 18

∧∨

Psalm 27:8-9

Your face, Lord, I will seek

When You said, "Seek My face," My heart said to You, "Your face, LORD, I will seek." Do not hide Your face from me; Do not turn Your servant away in anger; You have been my help; Do not leave me nor forsake me, O God of my salvation.

There may be times in the caregiving process when the reality sets in that your love one is passing away. It can be a time of great stress and sorrow or a special time that you share together at the end. This time may be many years away for you or it may be tomorrow, the fact is that the time will come. God will never leave you or forsake you, and He will guide you through. It is important to know when the time is right to discuss death, and how to prepare for it.

Are you clear on your loved one's wishes? Do you have an advanced directive that was completed ahead of time? Do you, your family members or representative have powers of attorney that can be used while your loved one is living and a properly witnessed will to govern the affairs afterward? Have beneficiaries for insurance been properly designated.

Do you have the information you need to compose an obituary such as where they went to school, what organizations they belonged to, the things they are most proud of and want remembered? What cemetery do they wish to be buried in or do they wish to be cremated? What is their favorite scripture? Most importantly, if they have not accepted Christ as their Savior, will they take the opportunity now?

These are not questions that you want to try to get the answers to in the final days. Ideally, this would be done years ahead of time. Many times we don't want to discuss this because we fear that it may make something bad happen or may give the impression that we want something to happen. Having these discussions ahead of time makes those final days much more peaceful because it's already taken care of. Now you can spend your precious time in peace with your loved one.

As the hours and days went by, mom knew that her time to see her Savior's face was drawing near. She wanted nothing more than to be with Him. I too had accepted that the time was coming near when in fact she told me. She began to float in and out of moments of reality and apparent disorientation. I say apparent as it was disorientation in my eyes, and that of my family, but I know it was all a part of the process of transition. I never quite knew what state she was in as she would say things such as, "Take those locks off of my feet so I can get up."

Of course there were no locks on her feet, but she was preparing herself to fly. She told me on one Friday that I should call her Pastor because she was going to die. Her vital signs were quite good, her output was good. She looked as well as she had in a few days. She then said something such as "Get those ducks out of here" so I smiled, and knew she was drifting in and out of reality.

Given that it was the weekend, I jokingly said, "Well mom, I will call the Minister, but it's the weekend, and I may not reach him so do you think you can hang around a little longer?"

She smiled and said, "Well, you'll have to ask Jesus that." We both smiled at each other, realizing it was somewhat amazing to be able to have this conversation without weeping, and with such peace. I told her I would call her Minister. She simply said, "Okay, that's good."

When I called her Pastor, who had faithfully followed her condition as had my Pastor, I said that my mother had expressed that she was going to die, and she wanted to talk to Him. He was on his way to a Christian education conference, and was nearly three hours away from us. He immediately said, "Oh, she is transitioning." While I knew this was the case, somehow hearing these words from his mouth made it official, and I had to pause for a moment. He said he would turn the car around, and he could be back in about three hours. I said, "No you don't have to do that, she just wants to talk to you now."

I also reminded him that, my mother, of all people would want him to go the Christian Education Conference because she was a defender of the faith. I asked if he would speak to her right then on the cell phone. He said yes, and pulled over the car. I put the phone on speaker, and took it to her room. I told her that her Pastor was on the phone. She smiled.

He began to talk to her, and a certain peace came over her. She was seeking her Saviors' face, and the Sheppard was leading her in grace. The last thing that her Pastor said to her was "If you get there before I do, don't crown Him until I join you"

Journal Reflections

✦ Take an assessment of the questions at the beginning of this devotional above.

✦ Take some time to determine where you stand with the many questions asked.

Devotion 19

⚡

Psalm 27:10

You are Never Alone

When my father and my mother forsake me,
Then the LORD will take care of me.

Blessed assurance, Jesus is mine! Caregivers may find themselves feeling isolated and alone. They may feel as though they are forsaken by everyone including the loved one who may no longer recognize them or want to hold long conversations.

The quiet and silence is not a rejection of you, but an opportunity for your loved one to prepare themselves for the journey ahead. The routine may change, and it may be uncomfortable, but rest assure, Jesus is there. He will smooth the path, and will take care of you and your loved one.

Frequently the literature that provides advice on the process of death speaks to the fact that the person may talk about taking a trip, they may become very introspective, looking for quiet and peace. I witnessed all of these stages as the days progressed.

My mother always loved to watch television. She loved game shows and mysteries. She watched every "Perry Mason" re-run with "Matlock" as a close runner up. All of a sudden, she did not want the television on, she wanted it quiet. Sometimes the quiet was uncomfortable for me because I am also one that likes background noise. I would say, "Mom don't you want to see "Wheel of Fortune?"

She would answer "No, not today."

Later that day, mom told me that she was going to get out of the bed and leave. This was an interesting thought since she had not been able to walk on her own for months. I asked her where she was going. She said, "I don't know, but I'm getting out of here."

I queried further, and said, "You must have some place in mind."

She said, "I'm going with my mother and father." I repeated the response as both her mother and father were deceased and she never talked much about her father. My grandmother had divorced and remarried my step grandfather long ago. I never knew my mother's father, and did not expect that she would have said she was going to him. I said, "Your mother and father are in heaven."

She replied "I know; that's where I am going."

I took this opportunity to explore her feelings on the topic, and repeated her words back to her "Oh, so you are going to heaven now?"

She said, "Yes."

I then followed with the question "How do you feel about that?"

She stated "Great, I feel great." We then begin to discuss heaven, the home waiting for her there, and how beautiful it would be. Regardless of the relationship with her earthly parents, she knew that her heavenly Father would be there no matter what.

Sometimes your mother and father have to leave you either because they proceeded you in death, they were not up to the task of being a mother or father, or they may be suffering from dementia and not even realize they are your parents. This thought of parents leaving us is very sobering.

David reminds us that no matter what, we are never alone. He believes this even though his own father did not always recognize his potential. He notes "When my father and my mother forsake me, then the LORD will take care of me" (Psalm 27:10). The assurance of the Lord's care bought such comfort to mom as she faced her last few days of life. She knew that she was never alone and that I would not be alone either. She was comfortable in the peace and quiet and the blessed assurance that Jesus was hers.

Journal Reflections

❖ What changes in routine have you noticed in your loved one's behavior?

❖ Have you been tolerant and respectful of these changes or have they been a source of discomfort? Just know that God will be with you and is in control, even in the time of change.

Devotion 20

⩗

Psalm 27:11-12
A Faithful Student

Teach me your way, O LORD, And lead me in a smooth path, because
of my enemies. Do not deliver me to the will of my adversaries;
For false witnesses have risen against me,
And such as breathe out violence.

*We will be faced with different adversaries though out the caregiving
process. These enemies of time, resources, patience and others will not
prevail against us if we have a strong foundation in Christ, and we
are sure of our salvation. This assurance in your salvation will help to
smooth your path regardless of your enemies.*

*The first step to achieving this salvation is accepting Jesus as your
personal Savior, trusting that you will have everlasting life if you believe
that he died for your sins, and that He was raised from the dead. It's so
wonderful to know that we serve a God that loves us no matter where
we are in the process of salvation, as long as we accept Him. We should
work daily to know Him more, and to love Him more.*

As the days progressed, I never knew which direction the conversation
might take, sometime very lucid, sometimes not. One morning I entered the
room with my usual "Hello mom."

She replied, "I'm getting out of here, this school is too expensive." I carried on the conversation with her asking, "What school?" She replied "I'm leaving this school because I'm finished learning."

I said, "Well mom you learn something new every day. I don't think we ever finish learning."

She replied "I've learned it all, and I'm finished learning." I thought about my reply, and realized that I was only half right.

We spend our lives going through the process of being saved. We believe, especially good Baptist, in the process of justification, sanctification and glorification. When I'm teaching this to my Bible students, I often frame it in terms of the past, present, and future.

Justification occurs when you accept the Lord as your Savior. You are made righteous at that very moment, not because of anything you have done. We are made righteous because of what happened in the past. Jesus Christ died for us many years ago so that we could be justified, and made right through His sacrifice of His blood for us all. We just have to accept Jesus as noted in Romans 10:9, "If you confess with your mouth the Lord Jesus, and believe in your heart that God has raised Him from the dead, you will be saved." It's not nearly as complicated as some make it out to be.

The next step in the process is known as sanctification, and that is the present. In sanctification, we work each day to perfect our relationship with Christ. We study his Word, and ask the Holy Spirit to teach us the way that we should go. We try every day to be more and more like Christ. On some days we do better than others. On some days we don't make the mark. We act in a way that would be displeasing to God.

Thank God for His grace, and His mercy. If we confess our wrong doings, He will forgive us because He loves us. We try to do better, and continue the process of sanctification. I always tell my students that while we try to perfect our relationship with Christ, we never achieve that until we meet Christ. Although we are not perfect, we keep working towards the mark, and we must always study and learn how God would have us grow in relationship.

As my mom talked about the school, I realized that she was telling me that she had reached the point of completion in her process of sanctification. At that very moment, she had learned it all; she had received all that God had to give her. There was nothing else for her to learn as it was now time for her to meet her Savior. She had proved herself worthy. School was over. No more learning needed to occur.

The last step in the process is called Glorification. This occurs when you meet the Savior face to face, and your salvation is complete. Mom was on the highway to glorification. I hope that one day I can say with the confidence that mom did, "I know it all. I've learned it all."

Journal Reflections

❖ Where are you in the process of salvation?

❖ If you have not accepted Jesus as your Savior, now is the time. Please accept Him right here and right now. After you have done this, pick up the phone or go to the Christian church of your choice, tell someone there that you have accepted Christ, and you want to talk to a spiritual leader about your decision.

❖ If you are already well grounded in your faith, then you are further along in the process, and you are in the sanctification stage. Consider how you can continue growing to find that perfect relationship with Christ.

Devotion 21

∧∨

Psalm 27:13
Don't loose Heart

I would have lost heart, unless I had believed that I would see
the goodness of the LORD In the land of the living.

*Caregivers are always busy doing something. We do, and then we do some
more. You may experience times when you really don't need to do anything,
but just be there. Just hold your loved one's hand, whisper a prayer, and
sit quietly. Ask them what they would like, and follow through.*

**While you are physically present in the transition period, you may need
to realize that this is a time when the primary interactions are between
your loved one and God. It is a time of peace. Sometimes your role is to
just stand. Stand with the confidence of knowing that the goodness of
the Lord can still be felt in the land of the living and His goodness brings
peace and comfort beyond all understanding.**

I came up stairs to my husband sitting on the couch busily working on the
laptop. He looked at me. He could see the tears in my eyes, something he
rarely saw. He asked, "What's wrong?"

I replied, "I don't know what to do."

"What do you mean?" he asked.

I said, "For the past few months, I have been very busy doing things. I have been turning, feeding, dressing, talking, crushing medications, and now, very little of this care is occurring. I am having such difficulty with this phase of "keep her comfortable." I can see that she is slipping away. There is nothing I can do to stop the process."

He held me close, and told me the same thing the social worker told me later that day. "The best thing you can do is to just be there. There is nothing left for you to do. This is between your mom and God now. Your job is to help provide the comfort and peace that she needs to complete her transition."

That day, I sat in her room all evening. She looked at me the entire evening without saying a word. She had a very pensive stare as if she were taking in my sight for the last time, knowing that she would not see me in this form again. She just stared.

I would approach her periodically and offer ice chips. She would take a few as her mouth was dry. I asked if she was in pain. She would say no. So I would just sit back down and "do" nothing.

Later that evening, my daughters came down to sit for awhile. We talked, we laughed, and they moved about. She didn't offer the usual smile that she does when they entered the room. They were clearly disturbed by this lack of response. I believe she was taking her last looks at them as well. Although she would have a different view of them from her new home, this was a view she would never experience again.

I went to bed that night with a famous song by Donnie McClurkin ringing in my ear. The words penetrating "What do you do when you have done all you can… you just stand." I knew I would just stand, and not lose heart. I knew of the goodness of the Lord. Just stand.

Journal Reflections

✢ Have you had those moments when you thought you had to do something, when in reality the best thing you could do is nothing?

Devotion 22

Psalms 27:14(a)
Not our Time, but His

Wait on the LORD

Many times we have things planned down to the minute. We have in our minds how certain things will happen and how we will react during a certain moment in our life. It is during the caregiving process that we learn that we must "Wait on the Lord." He will direct our path. We can plan, and we should, but the plan is not ours, but the Lords.

What a sense of comfort this brings as we do not have the pressure of making sure it's perfect. That is not our job. Birth is a miracle of God, and death is a miracle of God. Those that are not saved, die two deaths, a physical death, and a spiritual death. Those saved by God only die a physical death, but the spiritual death never occurs.

We had decided early on that when the final days came, we would transfer mom from home to the inpatient hospice facility. I had visited the facility several times. It was a beautiful and peaceful place. Each person had their own private room. The lighting and atmosphere was one of comfort for the patient and family. I envisioned that she would be moved to this facility, the around the clock staff would be there so she would never be alone, and they would ensure that she was always pain free. We would be there, likely in shifts, and we would have the support of the staff to guide us through the dying process.

This thought of a safe place to pass away was somehow a reassuring thought for both me and my family. My daughters had stated some fear of coming home without me being there, and finding that she had passed away. This was something they did not want to experience, and I didn't want them to experience this either. I wanted to honor their request since both my family and husband had been so generous in their time, opening up the home to mom and the myriad of workers that came in and out throughout the period of her illness. I wanted to be sensitive to everyone.

I expressed this desire to the nurse and social worker on several occasions, and they had noted this in the record. They told me they would do all they could to secure a bed in the inpatient hospice when the time came but that they could make no promises as no one could accurately predict that the time of someone's death, and the availability of a bed, would perfectly coincide. I understood this, and said we would do the best we could.

It had now become obvious that the time of death was fast approaching. The nurse made arrangements for mom to be transferred to a hospice room on Friday. Today was Wednesday. Her vital signs were still stable, and she was holding on. I prepared my family and told them that tomorrow, Thursday, would be mom's last day at home and that on Friday we would all meet at the hospice. I sent an email to my aunt and cousins with the address.

Everything was going as we had planned, perfect. I didn't tell my mom about the plans on Wednesday as I didn't want her to worry. I spent the whole day with her on Monday through Wednesday. My plan was to go into the office on Thursday morning and work one half day while the home aide provided her morning care. I would then come home from work on Thursday afternoon. I wanted to let her know that she would be moving to the inpatient hospice where she could get the best of care.

Thursday was a very strange morning. I tried to carry out my routine of getting mom straight, getting my coffee and bagel, and leaving when the home health aide arrives. This morning was different. I just couldn't decide whether to go or to stay. I dropped my perfectly prepared bagel on the floor. I spilled my coffee and fumbled about the house not knowing exactly what to do.

I went to turn on the television in mom's room so that she could listen to gospel on the cable channel that she usually listened to in the morning. A blue screen came on the television where the gospel channel usually appeared.

The blue screen had the words "no signal." I couldn't understand why the television in my mom's room had no signal, but every one of the others in the house did. I know now that there was not a signal because the spirit of God was the only signal that was needed in that room. His presence filled the room with such greatness that no other signal could get through.

I left for work leaving the home aide that had been so faithful. My middle daughter was also home. The hospice nurse would also be coming in a few hours to do her final assessment before the transfer. Just about noon the hospice nurse called me at work, and said that mom would not likely make it through the night. She said she would be moving her to the inpatient facility right away. I granted permission, and noted that I would be home right away.

My daughter did not know what was happening in the lower level in the in-law suite. Ordinarily, she would have gone down to see mom before going out. On this day, she decided to run a few errands first. I jumped in my car, and proceeded to go home. During my drive home, I received a call stating that mom had passed away.

I was only fifteen minutes away. My daughter had departed only fifteen minutes before. Mom utilized this small window of opportunity to slip away with none of us around. This was something she had to do on her own. This was something that had to happen in God's time, not mine. Until the end they were in control.

While I never told her that she was going to the inpatient facility, she had made up her mind that she was not going to go anywhere but to her heavenly home. No more stops for her. While many cherish seeing that last breath, I don't believe that she wanted me to be there for that moment.

What I remember is leaving her alive in a room filled with God's spirit, and my last words, as usual were, "Are you comfortable, can I get you anything?" Her response was "I'm fine."

Journal Reflections

✦ Are you prepared to go with God's plan?

✦ Are you prepared to wait on the Lord? It may be a perfect opportunity for you to practice giving the control to God on some small thing so that you can turn the large things completely over to Him.

Devotion 23

※

Psalm 27:14(b)

A True Act of Courage

Be of good courage. And He shall strengthen your heart;
Wait, I say, on the LORD!

*Every day that we wake up and begin to start our day, is an act of courage.
We never know what we will face as we carry out our responsibilities as
a family member, caregiver, and neighbor. Sometimes we are fortunate
enough to witness incredible acts of courage from others that inspire us.
Their lives serve as a living testimony to God's miraculous powers. We too
must tell our story so that we can serve as a living story of God's goodness.*

When I arrived home from my drive, the hospice nurse and nurse aide
awaited me. They hugged me, expressed their sympathy, and allowed me to
cry, but they seemed a bit impatient because they wanted to tell me about
what happened. They were very compassionate, gave me tissues, but I could
tell they just wanted to tell me what they had experienced. I thanked them
for being there, and said, "I was only fifteen minutes away." They reassured
me that she took leave of this world exactly when she wanted.

They began to tell me of an amazing experienced that they both witnesses.
I guess God put them both there so they could confirm each other's account.
They noted that they were in the room performing their medical care. They
were both standing in the room with my Mom, who at this point was saying
nothing. In the words of the nurse, she was "actively dying."

All of a sudden she began to talk, they listened, and recognized that she was praying. They said to each other, "Let's step out of the room so that we can give her some privacy." They both stood outside of the door. They could hear her talking to her Lord.

She continued to pray. Then they heard her say "Amen." They both heard the "Amen" and decided to go back in the room. When they went back in, she had gone to meet her Master. Amen in Hebrew meant "so be it." In modern day Christianity, "Amen" is used to affirm what is being said and to conclude a song or a prayer. Paul uses the word "Amen" to conclude all of his major epistles. In this case "Amen" was used as a courageous woman concluding her earthly life. She used the word to say so be it; I have come to the end of my journey here on earth.

Well done my servant! You have defended the faith, and you will enter into my Kingdom. The angels will welcome you, the trumpets will sound, the gates will swing wide open, and you will no longer be bound by the bed, or the inability to move. You are free, and you have earned your rest. No more crying, no more weeping, no more dressing changes, no more tube feedings. Hallelujah, Hallelujah, Amen and Amen!

As I walked into the room, the only thing that I could say was "She's beautiful." I must have repeated it at least three times. It is an odd thing to say as you look upon the remains of your loved one. These remains that had not yet been touched by a mortician were still beautiful. It's hard to explain this beauty; this restfulness; and this peace. Her spirit had moved on to her final home. Amen!

Journal Reflections

✦ Take the time to meditate on the goodness of the Lord, and our need to "Wait" on His Will. He will never leave us or forsake us.

✦ What thoughts come to your mind when you think of His goodness?

1

Devotion 24

ᐃᐧ

Psalms 27:4

The One Thing I Desired

One *thing* I have desired of the LORD,
That will I seek: That I may dwell in the house of the LORD
All the days of my life, To behold the beauty of the LORD.

An earlier devotional spoke of the "one thing," more in terms of the day to day desires. When David spoke of the "one thing," he specifically noted that there was really only one thing that is important.

As I addressed the thank you cards for all of the people that had been so kind during my mother's illness, and the time following her death, I had to include this scripture from Psalm 27:4.

It is the realization that there really is only one thing that matters, going to our eternal home. As they closed the casket at my mother's funeral, my oldest daughter continued to say "Thank you Lord, thank you Lord."

I later asked her what was going through her mind at the time. She said, "I was thanking God for putting such a wonderful person in my life. I thank God for taking her home as it was what she desired."

As we go about our task from day to day raising our families, seeking relationships and developing them, tinkering with our cars, pursuing careers, preparing our children for kindergarten, going to our club meetings, going to choir rehearsal and Bible study, there is really only one thing that ever matters.

Jean D. Moody-Williams

David had it right, and this is why my mother loved this scripture and requested that everyone read it when they visited. She understood this.

I can hear her saying…..

> [4] *One thing I have desired of the LORD,*
>   *That will I seek: That I may dwell in the house of the LORD*
>   *All the days of my life, to behold the beauty of the LORD.*

We love you, and remember, "Don't Crown Him until we get there!"

Afterward

Written by Hendri J. Williams

My mother-in-law, or mom as I fondly called her, has gone on to be with the Lord, but her example of how to live as a Christian left a legacy for our family as well as others. She clearly understood that in order "to contend for the faith that was once for all entrusted to God's holy people"(Jude 1:3), one had to develop a healthy faith in God. This is one of the most significant and greatest pursuits in a person's life.

Mom's healthy faith was nurtured and accomplished through Christian and spiritual disciplines such as praying, fasting, giving, teaching, worshiping, and loving. She loved the Lord with all her heart and desired the same for her children, grandchildren and the entire family. She loved me as a real son, and it was my pleasure to help my wife care for her in the last days.

As I watched mom's transition during those few weeks, I witnessed, even on her death bed, her unwavering desire to know the Lord more intimately. She was now positioning herself from Jude 1:3, referenced above to Psalm 27:4 –"One thing I have desired of the Lord, That will I seek: That I may dwell in the house of the Lord All the days of my life, To behold the beauty of the Lord."

The song that comes to mind when I think about mom is one that was written by Doris Akers. The lyrics to the song are "You can't beat God's giving, no matter how you try. Just as sure as you are living and the Lord is in heaven on high. The more you give, the more He gives to you. But keep on giving, because it's really true. That you can't beat God's giving no matter how you try." In other words, Mom's message was loud and clear. She knew that all she had was given to her by God. She also knew that the more one gives of themselves, the more joy they will experience in their lifetime. And let's be clear, the joy refers to that unspeakable joy that only comes from God the Father Almighty.

May God bless you and keep you and provide the much needed strength as you journey through this season of caregiving.

Resources for Caregivers

- Alzheimer's Association – www.alz.org –
  24/7 Helpline – 1-800-272—3900

- The National Association for Home Care & Hospice –
  www.nahc.org - (202) 547-7424

- Medicare Information – www.medicare.gov – 1-800-Medicare

- General Medicaid information - www.cms.gov/Medicaidgeninfo/

- The Association of Professional Chaplains - www.
  professionalchaplains.org –

- Caregiver Resources - www.usa.gov

- National Family Caregivers Association - www.nfcacares.org

- Hospital and Nursing Home Comparison Websites - www.
  medicare.gov/default.aspx

- Guide to Choosing a Nursing Home -www.medicare.gov/
  publications/pubs/pdf/02174.pdf

- Administration on Aging – www.aoa.gov

- Finding the right home care service - www.senior-inet.com/
  articles/article15.htm

- Guides to Long Term Care Insurance - www.aarp.org/money/
  insurance/

- AARP – www.aarp.org

CPSIA information can be obtained
at www.ICGtesting.com
Printed in the USA
LVHW040323080722
722994LV00001B/90

9 781449 753351